Living Lights

Fireflies in Your Backyard

Written by Nancy Loewen
Illustrated by Brandon Reibeling

Backyard Bugs

Thanks to our advisers for their expertise, research, knowledge, and advice:

Gary A. Dunn, M.S., Director of Education
Young Entomologists' Society
Lansing, Michigan

Susan Kesselring, M.A., Literacy Educator
Rosemount-Apple Valley-Eagan (Minnesota) School District

PICTURE WINDOW BOOKS
Minneapolis, Minnesota

Managing Editor: Bob Temple
Creative Director: Terri Foley
Editors: Nadia Higgins, Brenda Haugen
Editorial Adviser: Andrea Cascardi
Copy Editor: Laurie Kahn
Designer: Melissa Voda
Page production: Picture Window Books
The illustrations in this book were prepared digitally.

Picture Window Books
5115 Excelsior Boulevard
Suite 232
Minneapolis, MN 55416
1-877-845-8392
www.picturewindowbooks.com

Printed in the United States of America.

Library of Congress Cataloging-in-Publication Data
Loewen, Nancy, 1964–
Living lights : fireflies in your backyard / written by Nancy Loewen ;
illustrated by Brandon Reibeling.
p. cm. — (Backyard bugs)
Summary: Describes the physical characteristics, life cycle, and behavior of fireflies.
Includes bibliographical references (p.   ).
ISBN 1-4048-0145-6 (hardcover)
1. Fireflies Juvenile literature. [1. Fireflies.] I. Reibeling, Brandon, ill. II. Title.
QL596.L28 L64 2003
595.76'44—dc21
                                                                      2003006095

Table of Contents

Tiny Stars

Look! Over there. Tiny stars are winking and blinking in the tall grass by the river. They are fireflies.

5

Go ahead. Get closer. Be very still. Do you see what part of the firefly makes the light?

Fireflies use their lights to find mates. The males flash from the sky as they fly. The females flash back from the ground or grass.

There are more than 2,000 kinds of fireflies. Each kind has its own pattern of flashes.

A Firefly's Body

Catch a firefly, and put it in a jar. Do you see the two shell-like pieces on its back? Those are the firefly's hard outer wings. They protect the firefly's body.

Beneath the hard wings is a softer pair of wings. When a firefly flies, it spreads its hard wings apart and flaps its soft wings.

A firefly isn't really a fly at all. It's a beetle. True flies have one set of wings. Beetles have two sets—one hard and one soft.

Count the firefly's legs. Yes, six is right.
The legs can bend in several places.
At the tip of each leg is a foot with claws.
No wonder fireflies can climb so well!

Do you see those branches poking out of the firefly's head? They are antennae. The firefly uses them to touch and smell.

Look at those big eyes! Fireflies don't see clear images, but they're very good at seeing fast-moving things. This helps them fly away from enemies such as frogs and spiders.

Fireflies have compound eyes. Their eyes are made up of hundreds of tiny pieces. Each piece, called a lens, carries a slightly different picture. For a firefly, seeing is like looking into a cracked mirror.

15

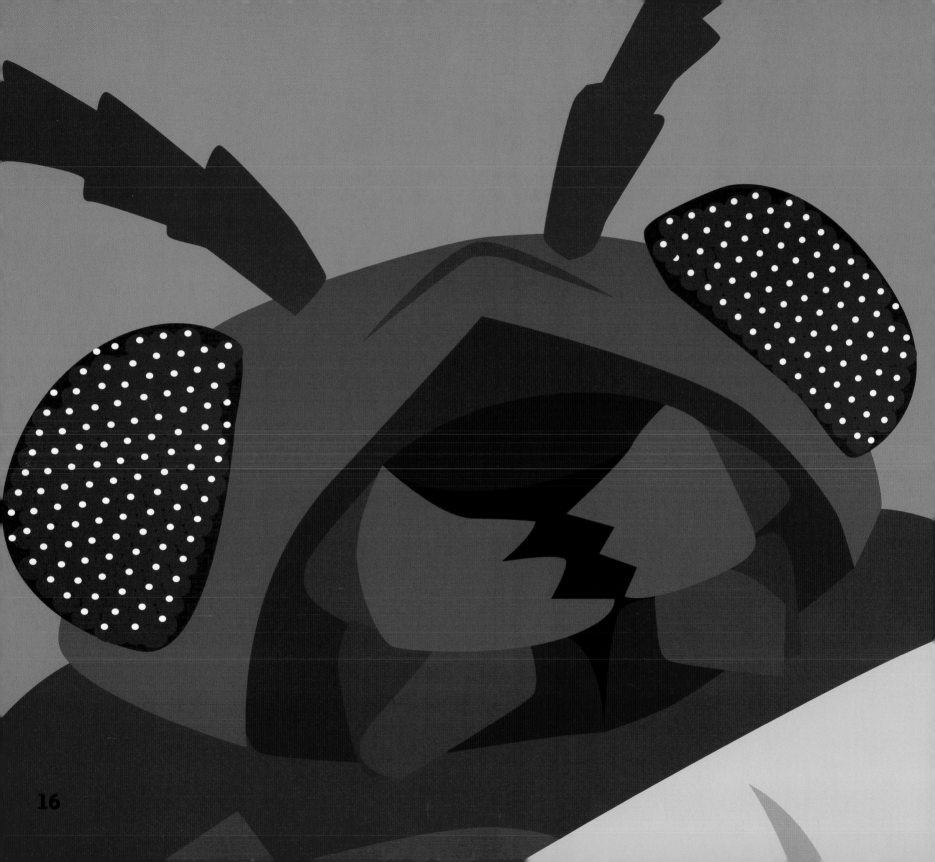

16

What Do Fireflies Eat?

If you look beneath the firefly's head, you'll see two little hooks. Those are the firefly's mandibles, or jaws.

You probably won't see a firefly eat. Most adult fireflies do not eat anything at all. Adult fireflies don't live long— just 5 to 30 days.

When a firefly first hatches from an egg, it is called a larva. A larva looks like a little worm. All summer long, the larva eats snails, insects, and earthworms. When the larva changes into a firefly in spring, it may not need to eat anymore.

Firefly Eggs

A firefly's main purpose is to mate. A female will lay as many as a thousand eggs in loose, damp soil. The eggs are small and round, and they glow faintly. Many of these eggs will become next year's fireflies.

Fireflies mate in marshes, swamps, rivers, and other damp areas all over the world. The insects live on every continent except for Antarctica.

Into the Night

Now it's time to let the firefly go.
The firefly will flash and fly a little
while longer. In daytime, it will hide
in the grass or under a leaf.

But it will be back tomorrow night,
making the evening a little bit brighter
with its dance of light.

Life Cycle of a Firefly

Like all insects, each firefly goes through an amazing life cycle. It completely changes its shape and form. It takes a whole year for a firefly to go from egg to beetle.

1. In summer, females lay eggs in damp soil.

2. After a month, an egg hatches into a larva. The larva looks like a little worm with ridges. It eats and grows all summer.

3. The larva burrows in the dirt. It sleeps in its burrow all winter.

4. When spring comes, the larva wakes up. It eats some more. Soon a stiff, white cover forms around its body. The larva is now a pupa.

5. After 10 days, the pupa splits apart. What is it now? That's right— a firefly.

Fun Facts

- In Southeast Asia, thousands of fireflies sometimes will gather in one tree, flashing their lights at the same time.

- A firefly's light is made by chemicals inside its body. Those same chemicals are used in light sticks—those glowing wands sold at fairs and parades.

- Sometimes a female firefly will copy the flash patterns of another kind of firefly. This fools the male of the different species into coming closer. Then the female eats the male!

- In some species of fireflies, the females have no wings. They sometimes are called glowworms.

- Like most insects, a firefly breathes through tiny holes on its lower body.

- To eat, a firefly larva squirts poison into its prey. That turns the prey's insides into liquid. Then the larva sucks up its meal.

Make a Glowing Firefly

Draw a big picture of a firefly, and cut it out. Then cut out a hole where the firefly would light up. Turn the firefly over. Tape a piece of tissue paper or plastic wrap over the hole. Hold up the firefly, and shine a flashlight from behind, through the hole. Your firefly glows!

Words to Know

antennae–Antennae (an-TEN-ee) are feelers on an insect's head. Antennae is the word for more than one antenna (an-TEN-uh).

compound eyes–Compound eyes are made up of lots of pieces, called lenses. These eyes are good for seeing fast-moving things.

larva–A larva is a newly hatched firefly. It looks like a little worm.

mandibles–Mandibles (MAN-duh-buls) are parts of a firefly's mouth that work like jaws.

mate–Male and female fireflies mate by joining together special parts of their bodies. After they've mated, the female can lay eggs.

To Learn More

At the Library

Carle, Eric. *The Very Lonely Firefly*. New York: Philomel Books, 1995.
Coughlan, Cheryl. *Fireflies*. Mankato, Minn.: Pebble Books, 1999.
Gerber, Carole. *Firefly Night*. Watertown, Mass.: Whispering Coyote, 2000.
Walker, Sally. *Fireflies*. Minneapolis: Lerner Publications, 2001.

On the Web

enature.com
http://www.enature.com/guides/select_Insects_and_Spiders.asp
Articles about and photos of almost 300 species of insects and spiders

The National Park Service
http://www1.nature.nps.gov/wv/insects.htm
A guide to finding and studying insects at national parks

University of Kentucky Department of Entomology
http://www.uky.edu/Agriculture/Entomology/ythfacts/entyouth.htm
A kid-friendly site with insect games, jokes, articles, and resources

Fact Hound
Fact Hound offers a safe, fun way to find Web sites related to this book.
All of the sites on Fact Hound have been researched by our staff.
http://www.facthound.com

1. Visit the Fact Hound home page.
2. Enter a search word related to this book, or type in this special code: 1404801456.
3. Click on the FETCH IT button.

Your trusty Fact Hound will fetch the best sites for you!

Index